Dedicated to Ted and Jennifer with love

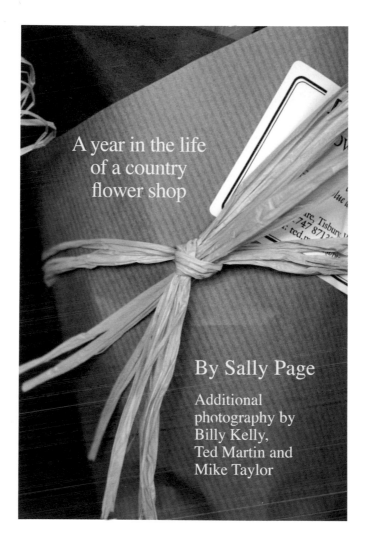

A year in the life
of a country
flower shop

By Sally Page

Additional
photography by
Billy Kelly,
Ted Martin and
Mike Taylor

THE FLOWER SHOP

Published by Half Full Press

Published 2007 by Half Full Press
1814 Franklin Street, Suite 440
Oakland, CA 94612
(800) 841-0873
(510) 839-5471

Printed and bound in China by C&C Offset Printing

ISBN: 0–9719552–7–1
ISBN: 978-0-9719552-7-1

Also available by Sally Page: The Flower Shop Christmas

For more information visit www.halffullpress.com
www.tedmartinflowers.com

If you have ever walked into a flower shop and thought
this is where I would like to spend some time –
then this is the book for you.

The following pages are a record of a year in the life of an English country flower shop and
through these we tell the story of the changing seasons and of the day to day life of the shop.

So, open the door, step inside, take a deep breath and immerse yourself in the fragrance and
colour of a village flower shop.

Introduction

To get to Ted Martin's flower shop you first have to find your way to Tisbury. There are four roads to choose from but all are small and winding, and in a snowy winter Tisbury can be more or less cut off for days, much to the delight of the school children. Take a road on an early spring morning and you will meander between gently rolling fields and woods perhaps catching sight of a lake or a mass of bluebells through the trees as you pass. Once you reach Tisbury you may well find yourself wondering "is this a village or is this a town?" But before you have had time to finish the thought you will have come down the small high street to The Square and be pulling up in front of the shop.

The shop has been observing life pass by in The Square in Tisbury for 150 years. At one time as a greengrocer's, once as a gentlemen's outfitters and at another time as a draper's. Now this old building looks out over The Square watching the seasons come and go, as flowers and plants are delivered into the shop from the markets. All the while the weather plays out its full variations against our window. Sitting amongst the flowers with a hot cup of tea is a good place to be when the wind is lashing the rain around The Square outside.

As the year passes the flower shop becomes quietly and discreetly intertwined in people's lives. We catch a glimpse of friendship, romance, birth and death. Customers may sometimes only make a small purchase but it is clear that flowers can, and do, make a difference to them.

There is a Chinese proverb that says "If you have two pennies spend one on a loaf and one on a flower. The bread will give you life and the flower a reason for living." As I walk up the street to buy some bread from the deli I can't help thinking that the Chinese are very wise. During the year we will take you to visit the deli and if I can find a third or a fourth penny – to the antique shop next door and to the new clothes shop in The Square. We will also take you out and about with us as we make deliveries, decorate homes and go in search of new flowers and plants.

We very much hope you enjoy your year in the flower shop as much as we did.

How would you like your tea?

Ted, as you might expect from the name, likes strong 'builders' tea. But images of grey haired ruggedness go out the window when customers and suppliers come face to face with our very feminine boss.

And I like my tea weak. But don't be surprised if I forget to drink it. Which, funnily enough, is rarely the case if someone pours me a glass of wine.

Jennifer is very particular about her tea. It may be for this reason, or because she just can't help looking after us all, that it is often Jennifer who goes to the kitchen first to put the kettle on.

January

A winter's tale

January in the shop

It is a fresh start to the New Year.

As I arrive in the shop after the Christmas holidays I see that Ted has hung a wicker wreath threaded with pussy willow on the door to welcome in the new year.

The planted bulbs are beginning to blossom on the windowsill in the cold winter sunshine and there is a feeling of anticipation in the air.

It is good to be back.

As I walk to the back of the shop with wishes of 'happy new year' Jennifer has just started unpacking the new delivery of flowers. Ted is busy carrying buckets of tulips and hyacinths onto the door step to decorate the front of the shop.

It is not long before the kettle is filled. Things are returning to normal.

An early customer, in from the cold, is a young dad with his hesitant rosy-cheeked children. They choose bunches of bright cheerful narcissi for mum, who is ill and is tucked up in bed at home.

A new customer comes into the shop. She has just moved into the area and is exploring the village with her young daughter Rosie.

Teddy wants to smell the flowers too.

"Rosie what is your teddy called?"

"Well I just call Teddy, Ted."

"Is Ted a boy or a girl?"

"Of course he's a boy, silly, he's called Ted."

In the flower shop we sell hand-made china from the Staffordshire potteries. The old pine dresser is packed with blue, white and pink plates, jugs and teapots. Many of our customers have started collecting the china, liking as we do, to mix all the colours and patterns together.

A jug filled with fresh flowers
is wrapped up with cellophane
and raffia ready for delivery.

January is sale time for the china. On a linen tablecloth we arrange an afternoon tea display with coffee cake and fresh bread from the deli. It is very tempting, but we are very good and do not eat the display.

On a rainy Friday, after a hectic week, Ted disappears for a while and comes back with a fresh coffee cake for us to eat.

Filling the shop with flowers

It always surprises me that this small shop, hidden away in a village amongst English hedgerows, should be such a window on the wider world.

Unpacking the subtly scented wax flower from Australia or long-stemmed roses from South America gives a glimpse of hotter and more exotic fields.

Armfuls of flowers that seem almost luminous in their freshness are piled up on the counter in a mass of contrasting colours.

My favourite are the tulips, which arrive wrapped in paper – fifty to a bundle.
I love seeing all fifty overflowing from a big glass vase or bucket.

As the seasons change so do the flowers. Of course nowadays it is possible to buy every variety of flower at any time of the year, however, Ted resists the temptation, preferring to see the shop shift with the seasons.

It is a real pleasure to be the first to pull almost forgotten seasonal flowers out of the boxes.

Often it is the scent that announces that these well-loved flowers have arrived. Whether it is the heady aroma of the hyacinths and narcissi, the sweet summer evening scent of stock or the woody smell of autumnal blooms.

Many of the flowers are delivered straight to the shop from the markets in Holland and England, whilst others arrive on large Dutch vans that act as mobile markets. Refrigerated to keep the flowers fresh, these lorries are cold to explore but are an Aladdin's cave for flower lovers. This is a good place to find unusual varieties and, sometimes, a bargain.

Whenever possible Ted buys flowers from local growers. These farmers and enthusiasts keep us supplied with sturdy plants, fragrant sweet peas and cottage roses.

Local people know we like to use interesting foliage and herbs and it is not unknown for us to find a bucket of rosemary left on our doorstep, or for us to be telephoned by friendly gardeners when they are pruning.

January: narcissi

According to an old saying you will have good luck for the year if there are narcissi blooming in your house as the new year begins.

This should make the shop a particularly lucky place to be.

flower shop secrets
FIVE ESSENTIAL VASES

If I could only have five vases at home these are the ones I would choose.

They look right in the places I want to position flowers and they are suitable for most of the flowers I am likely to use. They will cover the majority of occasions and, very importantly, they do not need hundreds of flowers in them to look good.

1. The bud vase
Good for your bedroom, a guest room or carefully placed near lighting it can create an inexpensive spot of colour anywhere in the house. Go mad and buy three of them and by lining them up you have a display for a side table or table centre.

2. The posy vase
This makes a pretty, informal table centre or it can be displayed by a bed or sit on a kitchen windowsill. By using a few colours mixed in with garden foliage you look like you have brought a country garden inside.

3. The medium vase

This is the size of vase that many people do appear to have in their homes and it is ideal for a display on a side table or on a dining table or kitchen table when not in use. By choosing one with a lip it helps direct the arrangement without being so wide at the top that the flowers flop outwards leaving nothing in the middle.

4. The tall slim vase

This is a great vase for when you are given or buy particularly long-stemmed flowers. By making sure you choose a tall vase with a relatively narrow neck you can get away with fewer flowers, but the display still looks impressive. In my case my tall slim vase is an old pasta jar, which is perfect for three stems of lilies.

5. The mini 'goldfish' bowl

I like this because it looks so good and the flowers seem to last so long in it. A hydrangea head will literally last for weeks, whilst roses seem to like bobbing around in the water. This vase is suitable for evening table centres, low coffee tables or even bathrooms.

From bump to baby

Arranging flowers to celebrate the birth of babies feels like a good way to start the year. This month it is the time for baby boys, although, rather appropriately, we do see the arrival of a Lily and a Daisy.

One of our favourite customers, Julie, brings her new baby son in to meet us.

Until a few weeks ago Julie was working in the village hairdresser's, a few doors down from us, and would call in for tea and a chat between clients.

It is a day for good news – we are asked to send flowers to another customer's best friend. She and her husband had been trying for a baby for many years and she has just announced she is four months pregnant.

Flora

Heather

Rosie

Jasmine

Daisy

Holly

Lily   Lavender   Marigold   Primrose   Blossom

January: hyacinths

flower shop secrets
HYACINTHS

When you trim the bottom of a hyacinth leave as much of the bulbous stem attached as you can, something within this part of the plant helps the hyacinth stay strong and straight. And as the fragrance of a hyacinth gets stronger the older it gets be careful not to throw them away too soon.

"The hyacinth's for constancy, wi its unchanging blue"
Robert Burns

Taking hyacinths home

more flower shop secrets

Hyacinths are poisonous and it is quite common to end up with a rash on your hands and face if you are not careful when handling them.

Delivering to the dairyman's cottage

February

February in the shop

The sharp sunshine of early February brings startling clarity to the winter countryside, before the days turn dismally grey and the rain sets in. The colours of the bright primroses and pale muscari help dispel the gathering gloom.

One wet lunchtime a woman wanders into the shop, she appears preoccupied and tired. We ask if we can help and after a long pause she admits that she is having a bad time at work and would just like to stand here amongst the flowers and think. We let her be.

I am just about to shut the shop when a young woman comes in with her baby. She buys herself some pink roses, she already has the wine and chocolates. Her husband has gone on a skiing holiday with some friends and she feels she deserves a treat.

Mangles and barrows

February: planting up

*"And all I longed for was one common flower
Fed by soft mists and rainy English air"*
Edith Nesbit

Jennifer is our expert planter. Give her a basket or old china bowl and she will soon have it brimming with plants. This time of year we have trays of spring bulbs arriving that she can't wait to get her hands on.

In the back room, hidden away from Jennifer, is a big box of tete-a-tete bulbs. These have been put aside for our near neighbour, Lord C who wants to plant them on his wife's grave. We remember Lady C very fondly. She and her husband would visit the shop together, frail and elderly, but laughing and bickering like young lovers.

The road to market

It turns so cold that the air takes your breath away. Ice forms in the buckets of flowers that are hardy enough to be still displayed on the street.

An early morning visit to the wholesaler means a scrabble in the dark for jumpers, boots and thermals.

As we are unpacking the flowers from market a customer places an early order for Valentine's Day. He will be away for a month in the Antarctic (which he assures us will be warmer than this). He is going there to study penguins. We find he is a penguin sculptor.

Generations of romantics

Young Love
I went to the shops with Sophie and Jane,
They said it was better with three.
I wanted to buy her a gun or a train
She meant that much to me.

I'd make her a bomb with a really big bang
And let her come into my den.
I'd share with her my worms and slugs,
My eggs from the tiny wren.

But Sophie said "No", that wouldn't do,
I'd have to do better than that.
And Jane didn't like my best idea,
To dig up the next door cat.

They told me that flowers would show that I cared
And picked out a really pink rose.
I suppose it's alright, if they carry the bag,
And promise that nobody knows.

When we got to the till, Jane had to pay,
As she moaned about scroungers and treats
"Just like a man," she said to her friend,
"He's spent all his money on sweets."

It is lovely to find that men can still be such romantics, whatever their age.

A young boy of around eight comes in flanked by his older sister and her friend to buy a rose for his 'girlfriend' – even though the girls end up paying.

The local thatcher wants to buy flowers for his wife and arrives clutching one of the shop's postcards. He asks for the flowers shown in the picture – *all* the flowers in the picture. Soon his spaniel has lost his favourite spot in the truck as we load up a huge glass vase crammed with stock, roses and larkspur.

One of our more senior, and very charming romantics, Mr Heaven has discovered the pale pink 'Heaven' rose. Heaven roses for Mrs Heaven. Perfect.

Getting ready for Valentine's Day

The roses start to arrive, but it will be a while before we see the men in the shop, leaving it, as they tend to do, until the last minute.

To help people choose we have photographed a number of ideas for Valentine's Day. They include red roses but also a hand-made pottery jug full of flowers and a bouquet of fifty tulips.

One customer, seeing all the flowers, asks us to put her husband on our mailing list for next year as she knows he never remembers Valentine's Day. I turn away to hide my smile. Her husband was in the shop earlier in the week and has ordered a dozen red roses to be delivered to her.

The night before

Our small side room is packed to bursting with orders ready to be delivered. Colourful raffle tickets are temporarily attached to them so we can easily identify the orders for the drivers.

The shop is a mass of roses and bouquets.

Valentine's Day

The early morning is a flurry of delivery drivers coming and going. Janet, our patient and always good-natured regular driver is the first to arrive. She is shortly followed by a number of friends who are pitching in to help out. I think they enjoy being there to see the reaction of people receiving the flowers, even if some addresses are very hard to find. By lunchtime most of the orders are out and the shop is calmer.

We pop out for more coffee and add a few shortbread hearts to the order.

Over lunch two builders come into the shop for flowers, one we know well. Now he has brought his mate in to buy flowers too. As he leaves he calls out that he won't see us again until this time next year. I can't help laughing. He does in fact come in regularly to buy his wife flowers, but clearly he does not want his friend to know this.

Laid back and scruffily attractive, a young man buys a single rose and asks if we sell rose petals. We don't, but I look around for a rose that may be going over which he can have; how many does he need? "Enough to scatter on the bed." I carefully bundle up six fully blown white roses for him, free of charge. Romance like this should definitely be encouraged.

49

February: in love with roses

Red roses are beautiful, but there is something disarming about a man who chooses a less traditional approach.

"The red rose whispers of passion,
And the white rose breathes of love..."

Cezanne

"But I send you a cream-white rosebud
With a flush on its petal tips;
For the love that is purest and sweetest
Has a kiss of desire on the lips"
John Boyle O'Reilly

Esperance

Cool Water

flower shop secrets
ROSES

If your roses get floppy, wrap their heads in paper so they are held upright, re-cut the stems and stand them in very hot water. Leave them there overnight and if they can be revived they will be by the morning.

more flower shop secrets

Always, always, re-cut your flowers before you put them in water. It may only take stems a few minutes out in the air to seal over, making it difficult for the flowers to drink. Cut them at an angle and you will ensure that they can drink as much as possible as the stems will not be resting flush against the bottom of the vase.

February 15th is my eldest daughter's birthday – a date I am unlikely to forget as she was born two weeks early after I had been on my feet all Valentine's Day in the flower shop I used to run in London. I cannot believe she is now sixteen.
Happy birthday Alex.

Delivering to the old church

March

March in the shop

March cannot seem to make its mind up. On the 1st of March there are blizzards, followed a few days later by spring sunshine, then it is back to the biting cold.

For a sixtieth birthday party we condition and prepare a number of arrangements for the tables. They are then packed together in a box for easy transport, a mass of tulips, narcissi, eucalyptus and wax flower.

Brides start to visit us to discuss their wedding flowers ready for the summer months ahead. The counter is scattered with photographs of bouquets, swatches of fabric and flowers, as we help them choose. One bride opts for creamy mini gerbera and roses mixed with cerise anemones to set off the pink tones in the terracotta silk of her dress.

flower shop secrets
GERBERA

Flowers with hairy stems, such as gerbera and anemones do not like to stand in deep water, they are much happier if just the bottom part of their stem is covered.

Spring rolls in

We are asked to deliver a spring bouquet suitable for keen gardeners to a couple who are in need of cheering up. She is disabled and he has just broken his leg. Perhaps, not surprisingly, there is no answer at the door, but we spot a crutch being tapped on the window and we are directed around the side of the house.

We receive a rush order for long-stemmed pink roses, each to be individually wrapped. Mr Howard, a local conductor, is performing at Salisbury Cathedral and wants the flowers for the young people in the choir who have worked so hard.

Spring baskets

"I need to take the flowers
in a bag,
in my basket,
in a box,
on my bike,
in a car,
on a train,
in a back pack,
on a plane,
in a fridge,
on a boat,
in my coat,
in secret,
with my seven kids
and the dog.

...will they be okay?"

flower shop secrets

If you are taking flowers on a long journey, choose a compact hand-tied bouquet with an aqua-pack. This can then be fitted into a straight-sided carrier bag which will help protect the flowers.

Ribbons & paper

Playing Shop
Crisp paper,
Raffia reel,
Boxy parcel,
Sticker seal.
Cellophane,
Organza bow,
Rainbow tissue
Row on row.
Slicing scissors,
Stamp it 'paid'.
Lost in thought
Of games we played.

Cards & messages

Making it special for Mother's Day

Mother's Day in the shop

Mother's Day weekend is the time for hot sticky coins and crumpled notes as we are handed carefully hoarded savings. Dads come in with children who, let loose, choose wild and unusual mixes of colours that may not quite match the home but will be especially well loved.

We fill a large basket with rose plants and lavender at pocket-money prices and the children can choose sheets of colourful tissue paper from our 'secret' cupboard for the gift wrapping.

I forgot to tell you
You are my sun, my moon and stars,
You are my world, my Earth, my Mars.
You are the road ahead of me,
You are my eyes through which I see.
You are the hand that leads my way,
You are my life through night and day.
You are my ground, my sea and sky,
You are the wings that help me fly.
You are my breath, heartbeat and all,
You are the catch beneath my fall.
You give me strength and help me swim,
You are the power that makes me win.
You are my dreams, you are my hope,
You help me laugh when I can't cope.
You are my clouds up in the air,
You are my spark, you are my flair.
You are the light beneath my door,
You are the one the sun shines for.
Libby Page

During Saturday, Ted manages to sneak a bouquet out to my waiting daughters, whilst I hide a bouquet in the side room ready for Jennifer's daughter Jo. And Ted isn't forgotten, her son Jack calls the shop to make sure she will also have a bouquet (that she hasn't had to make up!) for Mother's Day. We may all be florists but we still love being given flowers.

And as we are all mums the shop does not open on the Sunday.

Delivering to mums around the country

Many of our bouquets are sent by overnight courier around the country. One lady in Scotland who recently received flowers from us decides to send a bouquet to her Mum, who also lives in Scotland.

Other bouquets go to Wales, Yorkshire, Durham, London and Cornwall.

Stan, the driver who collects the flowers from us, has become a favourite customer of ours. He now orders flowers for his mum and mother-in-law and when he comes to collect them he brings his wife in to meet us. We feel we know her well as Stan talks so proudly of her and is often sending her flowers.

March: tulips

Tulips have been loved by people for centuries and I am no exception. I am constantly amazed by the variations in colour that you see. In the seventeenth century the Dutch used to scatter paint on the soil in the hope of creating new colour combinations. It was only in the 1920s that it was discovered that a virus carried by insects could cause tulips to naturally produce new colour strains.

flower shop secrets
TULIPS

If we have more tulips than we need in our delivery from market we store them at the back of the shop out of water for later. They do not mind this in the least. It also means this is a good flower to take to someone if you know they have to be out of water for a while.

flower shop secrets

If you don't want your tulips to get droopy, which they can do as they grow so fast in water, prick their stems with a pin just under the head and they will keep standing upright.

One regular customer buys some tulips to cheer herself up. She and her husband had a fire in their home and after months in a rented house they are moving back in. As she unpacks she finds that much of her favourite china has been broken whilst it was in storage.

We deliver a bouquet of tulips, anemones and roses to Trish in the pharmacy from one of the many people she helps – "Thank you for all your care and attention."

Delivering to Keeper's Cottage

April

Spring days

April in the shop

The days lengthen and the shop is filled with fresh spring sunshine. New china arrives and there is much cleaning, polishing and sorting.

We are asked to organise wedding party flowers for a couple returning from an around-the-world trip. They became engaged in Singapore, decided they couldn't wait in New Zealand and married in New York, before returning to a family celebration in their cottage nearby.

As we create an arrangement of roses and herbs and load up ornamental bay trees, a watching customer wistfully comments how, in another life, she would have loved to have had a flower shop.

We are often given only the vaguest directions for deliveries, perhaps the best being simply, "the cottage in the woods". Whenever we are in doubt the first person we ask is the local postman.

It is the turn of the post office to call on us. One of their staff is leaving and they ask us to arrange some flowers in the assistant's favourite coffee-time mug. In amongst the flowers we also place her post office badge.

A regular customer comes in to buy flowers for his wife who is in hospital. We suggest a small fragrant posy that can fit beside a bed and that is made up of flowers that can withstand the heat of a ward. He also takes armfuls of lilies to put in the house ready for her return home.

"Flowers leave some of their fragrance in the hand that bestows them."
Chinese proverb

flower shop secrets
FRAGRANCE

Many people ask for fragrant bouquets and this becomes especially important when the recipient is older and their eyesight is failing. Narcissi, hyacinths, stock, lilies and freesia are all good choices, but one fragrant flower that is often forgotten is the tuberose. This flower has the most wonderfully rich perfume and, as it comes from Mexico, it does not mind being kept in a very warm room.

Another gentleman comes in for flowers, this time for a funeral. The lady who died was a professor and a world-renowned expert on King Arthur. He tells us they would not be surprised if some mourners were to arrive wearing chain mail. He asks us to use red and white flowers as they have particular symbolism in Arthurian legend.

Towards the end of the day 'the lady who never smiles' comes into the shop. When I first served her I thought perhaps she was unhappy with the flowers or service, but she returns to us again and again, so I presume this is not the case. But however much we try we cannot get her to smile and we are all left wondering, what it is that makes her so sad.

April seems to be a time for apologies. We are asked to send flowers to a wife from a husband on behalf of their repentant dog. The card reads "I am sorry I ate the sofa. Love Rufus"

A young mum sends flowers to her mum on behalf of her sons who had been staying with their grandparents for the weekend. The message is "Grandma, we are sorry we infected you. Love Tom and Harry xx"

Welcome
to your
new home

During the spring we start to receive more requests for flowers for people moving home.

One local builder has a regular order with us. When one of his houses is ready and the new owners move in he sends flowers to welcome them.

As we suspect vases will be the last things to be unpacked from the boxes we suggest delivering jugs of fresh flowers as a pretty moving-in gift.

My new neighbours
On moving day they looked impressed,
They said, "she sure knows how to dress."
I rather think they liked my hats,
The wedding ones, too large to pack.

Easter

During Easter weekend there is a constant stream of customers through the shop. Some are taking flowers to friends or relations they are staying with, others want flowers for the house as they have guests arriving.

With chocolate eggs and bunnies by the till we are proving very popular with the children. I am glad to hear one older lady tell a sick-looking little boy that chocolate is very good for you, especially if you have a cold.

April: out and about at Neal's Yard

Every week customers Tom and Mark buy flowers for their shop and consulting rooms in Salisbury. We always enjoy their visits, as we catch up with the progress of the lambs at home on their small-holding. They also provide advice and interesting products for us.

Lilies are a favourite choice as they last well under the lights and add to the fragrance of the shop.

flower shop secrets
LILIES

Lilies last longer if the pollen is removed as this tricks the flower into thinking it must bloom for longer. Use a tissue to pinch off the pollen, but be careful not to get it on your clothes as it stains. If you do get lily pollen on your clothes do not try to brush it off or remove it with water, this only makes things worse. Instead, use Sellotape to remove the pollen by gently dabbing it.

April: a visit to Compton Marbling

Situated in a quadrangle of nineteenth-century stone barns, Compton Marbling is a specialist handmade paper company run by a charismatic woman, Solveig Stone. We have got to know Solveig over the years as she frequently buys flowers for friends and family.

Four times a year Solveig also runs busy and interesting craft fairs from her barns. For the April fair we provide flowers for the tea room and run a charity draw for a bouquet of flowers.

When the draw takes place we are all pleased to see it has been won by a lady we know.

Sadly it was only a few months ago that we were asked to prepare flowers for her husband's funeral. Within the tribute we were asked to represent countries he had associations with, such as Scotland, South Africa and Pakistan. We included thistles, freesias and Gloriosa lilies amongst the flowers.

April: iris

In some languages iris means 'flag', and in the past they were used as a symbol for kings going into battle. Hence the origin of 'fleur-de-lys' in heraldry.

Miss Ellis calls us, she is looking for white irises which she needs for a church display. Her car is out of service so we run the flowers over to a neighbouring village for her. The irises have been standing in the rain and look wonderful with the rain droplets clinging to their petals.

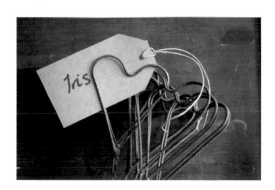

Delivering to Payne Place House

May

May in the shop

Spring passes and we welcome the arrival of early summer flowers. The shop becomes a jumble of pinks, lilacs and blues.

Sue, who owns the local hairdresser's, calls in with good news. Her daughter has just gone into hospital to have a baby. This will be Sue's second grandchild. She is back later on with a request from her eldest granddaughter – could we make a pretty posy for mummy and her new sister.

In May the local church holds a musical weekend and the Tisbury flower group create a flower festival in St John's, using the theme 'a symphony of flowers'. We supply some of the flowers and when the shop is closed we all visit the church. It looks amazing. Each display is different and a huge amount of work has gone into them. I particularly like a sweeping display of lilies and deep-green foliage on the font.

A wreath of lisianthus, stocks and phlox

flower shop secrets
TABLE CENTRES

Standing a hurricane lamp in a wreath of flowers is a simple way to create a table centre. It also has the advantages of being suitable for outside and does not need masses of flowers in it to look good. In this case we combined four types of foliage with four stems of flowers plus some lavender snipped from a plant. These were all arranged in an Oasis wreath.

May: peonies

Meaning: most beautiful

One of our friendly gardeners, Pat, is passing the shop and we ask her in to see some of the peonies that have just arrived. We know she has some beautiful peonies in her own garden. She explains that the cutting for these deep-red flowers was given to her by a family friend. The friend told her that as they would bloom again and again he would always be with her in the garden, which, since his death, she takes particular comfort from.

flower shop secrets
PEONIES

If your peony heads are very tight and they do not look like they will open, rinse the heads in cold water as this can help release the petals.

Ted

Ted's real passion for flowers started in her cottage garden at home. When visiting friends she would cut flowers and foliage from her garden and tie them into natural fragrant posies as gifts. These friends encouraged her to take her interest seriously and she soon started to arrange flowers for friends and neighbours.

A friend also took a hand when she saw a shop for rent in Tisbury and persuaded a very nervous Ted it was just what she needed. It was not long before she opened the doors of Ted Martin Flowers.

Now in the early summer Ted is out in her garden making the informal rambling posies that she loves, ready for her favourite earthenware jug on her kitchen table.

Friendly flowers

Many of the flowers and messages we send are all about friendship. Flowers can say, "I've remembered" "I am thinking of you" "I am so pleased for you". And sometimes, when friendship goes awry, they can say "I am really very sorry I got it wrong".

"The Rat stared straight in front of him, saying nothing, only patting Mole gently on the shoulder. After a time he muttered gloomily, 'I see it all now! What a pig I have been!'"
Kenneth Grahame

Two women are in the shop browsing and whilst one of the ladies is turned away looking at the china her friend buys her a posy of phlox and veronica that she'd been admiring.

A lady orders a bouquet for her friend who was due to fly off on holiday today. Her friend's daughter has just broken her arm and her friend feels she will need help at home with the children and so has cancelled her longed-for holiday.

A high proportion of the customers who send flowers are women and it is sometimes a struggle to persuade men that sending flowers does not mean they have done something wrong!

Different worlds

She hopes for flowers and a chocolate cake,
His cold coffee-mug rings tomorrow's date.

She spies a small package hidden in the car.
He knows the new plugs can't have gone far.

She talks of the flowers she once tried to grow,
He's sure the soil's missing deoxy-phango.

Her sigh shimmers through the spirit level glass.
If she needs a new shelf she only has to ask.

He hammers as the radio plays their special song,
He'd like to send flowers but she'd think
                                    something's wrong.

Friends and neighbours

Next door to the shop is The Old House, a very tempting antique shop, full of interesting things that we are sure we can't do without. If Jennifer is missing it is quite likely we will find her there, just having a quick look at what has recently arrived.

If Ted is missing she may well be further down The Square in Amorrio … just checking whether they have it in her size …

... and if we fancy nice bread, cheese and wine, the Old Forge deli is only a short stroll up the hill ...

May: herbs

A customer looking for a moving-in present chooses a selection of herbs which we then plant into a ceramic trough suitable for a kitchen windowsill. The scent of the herbs fills the shop.

We all enjoy using herbs in bouquets when they are in season. Flowering mint, flowering oregano and rosemary are mixed in a bunch to be sent to a keen cook who is having a bad week.

flower shop secrets
HERBS

We use fresh herbs that also dry well to make natural wreaths for our kitchens that can then be picked and snipped at as we cook. To do this we wire the herbs into bunches and then wire them onto a light circular metal frame. Good herbs to use are rosemary, bay, oregano and thyme.

May: Lizzy to her friends

Lisianthus are beautiful flowers that come in the softest of pastel colours. They are very good for arrangements as they often have several individual flowers on a stem, although we are careful not to get water on the petals as we work with them since water spots can make the flower go mouldy.

A posy of pink lizzy, roses and snapdragons

Delivering to Duck Street Farm

June

June in the shop

In June the hedgerows bloom with rosebay willowherb and cow parsley. Lupins grow tall in the sunshine, peeping over garden hedges.

We deliver flowers to a gentleman who, we recall, was widowed a few years earlier, leaving him to bring up his daughter on his own. We are now delighted to be arranging wedding flowers for him.

Can you have too many flowers?

A young boy comes in to buy flowers for his mum's birthday, he proudly announces he is going home to bake her a cake. He is filled with confidence, which we secretly hope is not misplaced.

We start to receive requests for summer parties, including a large order from a family who are throwing a retirement party for their farm manager.

The breeze is warm and the late afternoons are sunny and balmy as I drive home from the shop.

The road home

Apron
Strings

June: snapdragon and stock

Snapdragon and stock always remind me of herbaceous borders and of the scent of a summer garden at dusk.

These were the gardens of my childhood with fragrant lines of new cut grass, old fashioned bird baths and borders of pinks and marigolds. If you were to carry on down the garden and slip behind the beech hedge you then found yourself in a world of canes, vegetables, compost and, if you were lucky, strawberries.

flower shop secrets
FLOWER CARE

To help flowers last longer strip the lower leaves
off so they are not immersed in water. This helps
prevent bacteria forming. For the same reason it is
also important not to bash or hammer the ends of
flower stems.

Delivering flowers

"You know where to deliver to, you went there the year before last"

TED MARTIN
Flowers and China
The Square, Tisbury

01747 8
07939 2

flower shop secrets
DELIVERIES

If you are taking flowers to someone by car, keep them in a bucket of water as you travel. We use rectangular buckets rather like the ones you can buy for mopping floors, as they are much less likely to tip over than round buckets.

June: summer party

We are asked to prepare flowers for a fortieth birthday party. After a week of rain the day of the party turns out to be bright and sunny. A marquee stretches from the house across the lawn next to the kitchen garden.

We find a shady spot under the trees to make up the arrangements and spend a very happy afternoon filling a mixture of modern and traditional vases and china with peonies and roses.

It is mid-afternoon before we remember we haven't really stopped for lunch and have an impromptu picnic on the grass.

Pink glasses are lined up on the bar ready for the champagne.

We carry the flowers into the marquee and arrange them in informal groups in the centre of the tables.

The day is warm and we can tell that the evening will be still and fine.
We later hear that the party was a great success.

"If a June night could talk it would probably boast it invented romance"
Bern Williams

Delivering to Chilmark House

July

Summer blooms

July in the shop

A ribbon of girls in green-and-white checked dresses stream down the steps from the school bus that pulls up in front of the shop. These are days of glorious soft sunshine from cornflower skies.

On the fourth of July we take a call from the States ordering a red, white and blue bouquet, to be delivered locally, with the message 'Independence rules!'

Two girls come in from the local high school, friends of Ted's son Jack. The girls have ordered arrangements of white and cream flowers for their prom. We load up the flowers in boxes and crates for them and help them out to the car.

As the school year draws to an end we receive many requests for 'thank you' flowers for teachers, including, "To Mrs Jones, the one and only."

flower shop secrets
CUTTING

If we use flowers and foliage from our gardens we cut them early in the morning or late in the evening as this is when the stems will have the most water in them.

To keep them in the best condition we then put them in a bucket of water for several hours before we arrange them. This is especially important if you are working in Oasis.

To see the different looks we might achieve with the same flowers, Ted, Jennifer and I each arranged a similar bunch of flowers, as we might do at home.

We base the bunch on nine stems of flowers, as this could be what a customer would buy in the shop to treat themselves for the weekend. We chose three stems of purple larkspur, three stems of lilac stock, and three creamy lisianthus. We are also allowed to add a bit of foliage from the garden.

Odd numbers
It is easier to get a balanced and pleasing effect with an odd number of flowers, so we often build up arrangements using 3, 5, or 7 stems of one flower type. Of course this rule goes out the window if someone sends you a dozen roses.

Different levels
By arranging each flower type at a different height in the container you give your arrangement depth and interest.

Sally: I chose a slim vase so my bunch will create some impact in a tall room against a pale sitting room wall. To add to the fragrance and to fill in some gaps I add a few stems of apple mint.

Jennifer: Using a pottery jug Jennifer wants to create a natural country bunch for her kitchen table. This arrangement is going to be seen from all sides so she arranges her flowers like a posy. Alchemilla mollis adds to the natural effect.

Ted: Finding a basket she likes, Ted wants a slightly more structured arrangement for a wooden chest in their snug at home. She frames her bunch with hosta leaves from her garden and adds some variegated pittosporum to bring out the cream of the lizzy.

July: summer weddings

The weekends are busy with wedding work and sometimes extra help is needed. Jill, a very talented local flower arranger is called in to help. She is part of a group called the Chalke Valley Dozen, which she laughingly explains is not based in the Chalke Valley and has more than a dozen members, but this informal group of friends all pitch in to help each other when families are arranging large parties or weddings.

Wedding work means an early start as we cut and condition the flowers before we make up posies, buttonholes and corsages.

flower shop secrets
IN THE FRIDGE

We keep buttonholes and corsages in the fridge to keep them as fresh as possible and always advise people to do the same once they get them home.

A slightly harassed and hung-over best man comes in to collect a bouquet the groom is sending to his bride on the morning of their wedding.

He's followed by the father of the bride who is collecting the three bridesmaid's bouquets of roses, scabious and lizzy. We help him carefully load the box packed with tissue paper and flowers into his car.

A few hours later the best man is back, looking rather sheepish. He doesn't know how to tie his cravat, can we help him?

Decorating the marquee: Looking at the rain, hoping for the sun

And the sun does shine

A bridegroom collects a box of rose buttonholes

*"Grow old along with me
The best is yet to be."*
Robert Browning

"Dad, please hold
my flowers for a
moment"

Beautiful bridesmaids

146

"We live in our own world,
A world that is too small
For you to stoop and enter
Even on hands and knees"
R S Thomas

147

Country flowers for a country wedding

Delivering to Ivon House

August

August in the shop

The tractors rumble past the shop and the way to work can be slow if you get behind a combine moving slowly between fields. The countryside is striped gold where they have been working.

A lady walks up from the train station and buys a vast bunch of crimson freesias for her mum who lives in Tisbury. She is on a visit from her home in Montreal and is nearing the end of her long journey.

On the same day we are visited by a very cheerful older couple on a day out. They explain that if they stay at home they end up working, so have decided instead to come out to play.

We take an order for a golden wedding anniversary and choose eremurus, dahlia and rudbeckia for the bouquet.

"Dawn love is silver,
Wait for the west;
Old love is gold love –
Old love is best"
Katherine Lee Bates

152

Some weekenders who have seen flowers that we used to decorate the local pub for a celebration of a civil union, ask us to prepare some flowers for their own special event.

The hospital bucket

In a corner on her work bench Jennifer keeps the hospital bucket. Here she stores the flowers she rescues, those with broken stems or blooms that seem to be just past their prime. Small stems of foliage left over from our arrangements also find their way there. She will not let us throw anything away.

We use these flowers to fill jugs and vases for display in the shop and also sell 'bits posies' at sale prices for people wanting a bargain. Made up of a mishmash of flowers and colours, I think these are some of the prettiest posies we prepare.

Jennifer

Jennifer, like Ted and I, has had many careers in her life. In the past, Ted was a nurse, I have worked in research, whilst Jennifer has been a nanny, a doctors' receptionist and, with a keen eye for a bargain, she has also bought and sold furniture.

Nowadays she keeps her hand in by running a craft fair locally for the National Trust and she still buys pieces of furniture that take her fancy, which she then strips and paints. Some of these she sells and those she can't bear to part with she keeps for her own home.

The sweet pea man

On the edge of the New Forest, in his garden and on his allotment Dave Manston grows sweet peas. He has grown sweet peas since he was nine years old, and he won't mind me saying, that this was some time ago.

I drive over to buy some fresh cut stems for a special order and the car is filled with the most wonderful scent as I drive back over the downs to the shop.

These are beautiful flowers and Dave has won many awards for them over the years, including prizes at Chelsea Flower Show.

"Our England is a garden, and such gardens are not made
By singing: 'Oh, how beautiful' and sitting in the shade"
Rudyard Kipling

August:
all white

flower shop secrets
COLOUR

Many people struggle to decide which flowers they should put together for a gift, so if people are un-sure we often suggest sticking to one kind of flower or recommend choosing flowers that are all the same type of colour.

One combination that always looks good is to mix white and cream flowers together with interesting foliage.

On one day we receive two orders for all white flowers, one is for a first anniversary and the second is for a couple who have been married for thirty-two years.

Anniversary

"Bring me flowers when I am old
And in long shadows hide.
Fill my arms with garden roses,
As you did for that young bride.
The years may take us travelling,
Steps so close we cannot see.
Sweet scent remembered,
Your roses next to me"

Anon

Summer christening

A lovely customer, Samantha, comes in to arrange flowers for her grandson's christening. Her son lives in Australia and she did not for a moment expect that she would be able to host the event over here.

She is planning a real English christening, with delphiniums, cream tea and strawberries. She clearly cannot wait for her family to arrive.

August: delphiniums

We gently unpack long stems of delphiniums in shades of purple, lilac and blue. A few stems break off and Hannah, our old Saturday girl who is home for the holidays from university, wires them, as she has seen us do, and tucks them into her hair.

There is something about Hannah ...

flower shop secrets
DELPHINIUMS

If delphiniums do break you can cut them down and
fill a smaller vase with pieces of the stem for a more
compact display.

Harvest

For late summer weddings we include wheat, oats and barley in some bouquets. On the way home from the shop the evening light is low and golden over the fields.

flower shop secrets
GLASS

If glass vases have crusty water stains that cannot be washed off we fill the vases with water and drop in one or two Steradent tablets and leave them overnight. In the morning the stains are easy to wash away.

"Now came fulfillment of the year's desire,
The tall wheat, coloured by the August fire"
William Morris

Delivering to the Horseshoe Inn

September

September in the shop

September brings crisp sunny mornings with an elusive hint of autumn. By the afternoon the air in the shop is warm and fragrant again. The last refrain of the passing summer.

The sunshine brings out our neighbours. The ironmonger, greengrocer and garage owner call in for help with just-remembered birthdays and 'thank yous'.

Freesias, sunflowers and lilies fill the main table. Golden yellow and ochre they give a taste of the autumn to come.

Reverend Bickersteth telephones us. Before he retired, John Bickersteth was the Bishop of Bath and Wells, he also edited a fascinating and poignant book comprising the letters of his uncles who fought in the First World War. The Reverend Bickersteth's sister has died and he would like to order yellow rose buttonholes for all the family attending the funeral service as a way of celebrating her life.

As we unpack fluffy lemon mimosa from the box I know autumn is on the way. Its slightly sweet mustardy smell takes me back to my first job in a flower shop. I worked as a Saturday girl in a shop near Hampton Court Palace for a lovely, mad, whirlwind of a woman called Tweazle Jones.

Soft blues and lilacs give way to stronger colours, as hazy purples mix with vibrant pinks and reds.

A lady orders a beautiful vivid bouquet on behalf of her brother, who is abroad, for his girlfriend's surprise birthday party. We give her a card so her brother can write his own personal message. We later find out that his 'message' is a proposal of marriage.

Baskets

Baskets are delivered into the shop in enormous cardboard boxes. Just when I think we cannot possibly get any more boxes into the shop the driver unloads the last of them. The baskets are unpacked and piled up on any available surface, and on a few unavailable ones too, as we check them off the list and write the price tags. A keen woody fragrance fills the shop as I delve in to pull the last basket out.

September: birthdays

Orders for birthday flowers keep us on the go most of the year and in September the shop gets ready to celebrate its own birthday with champagne and cake for the customers – and for us.

"Flowers really do intoxicate me"
Vita Sackville-West

One of our regular customers Amanda asks for our help with her husband James's fortieth birthday. He thinks he has twenty or so guests coming for a rather staid dinner party, but Amanda has other ideas. She has discovered a company who will turn a room in your home into an exotic Bedouin tent complete with silk hangings, cushions and lanterns. This seems like much more fun. We suggest we use tall shimmering containers filled with ginger and ornamental pineapples to match the surroundings.

September: freesia

Freesias were some of the first flowers that I was aware of. As a child I knew my mum liked their scent and when my dad bought her flowers he would often chose freesias for her. Now, when I smell freesias in the shop it always makes me think of my mum.

flower shop secrets

FREESIAS

Customers often choose freesias because of their wonderful fragrance. However, not all varieties of freesias are heavily scented, for example, some white freesias hardly smell at all. If you love the scent of freesias the pink and red varieties tend to be the most heavily perfumed.

September in September

Flower pots, champagne bottles, teapots

We use all sorts of containers for flowers, not just vases, baskets and jugs. Here are three we particularly like.

flower shop secrets
CONTAINERS

This may seem obvious, but you can always put a watertight pot inside a fragile and more attractive container. In the shop we are often looking for new ways to display the flowers and may well grab a chipped vase or battered pot, wedge it in a beautiful basket or terracotta pot, and then fill it with flowers without bothering to line the container or get the Oasis out.

Delivering to Lime Tree House

October

Autumn falls

October
in the shop

As October mists creep into the valley, customers appear to be drawn to the warm rich colours of autumn. We are kept busy making up hand-tied bouquets packed with burnt orange, red and rust coloured flowers. We hardly touch the pale pastel tissue paper and reach instead for brown, purpley-grey and even lime-green tissue to set off the autumn shades.

The late afternoon sun that now sits low in the sky lights up the banks of flowers. A new rose arrives called 'new fashion'. With a red centre and almost gold outer petals it appears a perfect complement to the season.

We have a rush order for two seasonal bouquets. One is going to a lady with cancer – the customer would like to take it herself but has a cold and does not want her friend to catch anything that could interfere with her hospital treatment.

Another is going by overnight courier to a colonel as a 'thank you'. I make the mistake of assuming the colonel is a man, but find out my error in time.

Smooth orange pumpkins and grumpy looking gourds are piled in baskets at the front of the shop amongst the ivy and red and yellow pepper plants.

The end of a long autumn day

Saying 'thank you'

thank you for lunch thank you for the loan of the piano thank you for collecting the children thank you for looking after the dog thank you for such a great holiday thank you for being you thank you for my new car thank you for watering the plants thank you for the party thank you for supper thank you for having us around again thank you for the tickets thank you for the good wishes thank you for the loan of the villa thank you for a fabulous weekend thank you for minding the cat thank you for saying yes thank you for taking part thank you for being there thank you for the Christmas puddings thank you for your help thank you for the horse box thank you for everything thank you

"Thank
you
for
not
posting
my
letter"

"Thank you for catching the rabbit"

October: cabbages

cabbage *n.* **1a.** any of several cultivated varieties of Brassica oleracea, with thick green or purple leaves forming a round heart or head. **b.** this head usually eaten as a vegetable

**Usually,
but not always ...**

cabbage *colloq. derog.* a person who is slothful and inactive or lacks an interest

October: from cabbages to orchids

flower shop secrets
ORCHIDS

The way to an orchid's heart is to ignore it. These beautiful flowers often suffer because they are over-watered. Only water your orchid every other week, standing it in water for half an hour or so. When it has had a drink place it on the draining board to let any excess water seep away so the roots are not left soggy.

Sally

I have always wanted to learn to draw, even though I am pretty sure I don't have any great talent. I have occasionally looked into courses but either they were too far away or I was busy with work. Or maybe that has been my excuse.

At other times I have thought I should just draw something. But what?

And then I mentioned this to one of our customers, John, who does attend a local art group. John is a widower who visits us to buy roses in memory of the flowers his wife loved. John took me to task and decided it was high time I had a go.

So now on a Wednesday, John calls in to inspect my latest effort and to tell me what to draw for the following week.

Thank you John.

Delivering to the village school

November

November in the shop

With November comes a hard frost. Overnight the coutryside turns from golden brown to spectacular scenes of silver and white. In the morning, as we open up, the shop is icy but by the afternoon it is warm and cosy in the fading light.

flower shop secrets
ALL SAINTS

November the first is All Saints Day. This is not really celebrated in England but it is in many other parts of Europe. As a result the prices of flowers are always high at the beginning of November.

When we are not tucked away in the warm we are out and about delivering locally.

One of the gardeners, who drops in with foliage, has discovered the effect of flowers (he will not accept payment from us, so as a 'thank you', we have been giving him flowers for his wife). He now places an order for a bouquet for her.

Lady Margadale has a number of house guests and we make up the flowers for the bedrooms and dining rooms.

A lady needs a pretty feminine posy for a funeral. Her old nanny who used to be a ladies' maid at the nearby stately home has died aged 92.

The language of flowers

"We only understand death for the first time when he puts his hand upon one whom we love"
Madame de Stael

Seeing new babies arrive or helping to celebrate anniversaries and birthdays is wonderful, however it would not be complete without being there for people when someone dies.

In the face of someone's grief, offering tea and tissues, as we sometimes find ourselves doing, can feel like a feeble response, but when we start to talk about flowers it really does seem that we are helping.

People often choose funeral flowers to express how they felt about the person who died or to recall something about them. At these times flowers really can speak to them and for them.

Living in a small community means that sometimes we are personally involved. We may well know who has died or feel we have got to know them as we have delivered flowers to them during a long illness.

Thomas Osmond the local clockmaker was a neighbour of ours. In the 1800s he lived in Clock House just behind the shop.

Rosemary for remembrance

November: hydrangeas

These beautiful flowers always make me think of autumn days and of wood smoke, especially those with misty blue and purple heads.

"So dull and dark are the November days,
The lazy mist high up the evening curled"
John Clare

flower shop secrets
HYDRANGEA

Hydrangeas can become disappointingly limp very quickly. This is usually easy to fix. Put a few inches of boiling water in a jug, re-cut the stems and stand the hydrangeas in the hot water for 30 minutes to an hour. Wrap the heads loosely in brown paper or newspaper as you do this to protect them from the steam. After the stems have had a chance to really open up put them back into cold water.

more flower shop secrets

Hydrangeas make a wonderful display on their own in a large vase or jug, but if you find they are too big for your room you can always take just one and tuck other flowers and foliage in amongst the petals for a smaller posy.

To dry hydrangeas we would not recommend hanging them upside down or leaving them without water. Our best results have been achieved by keeping them in an inch or so of water in a warm room and allowing them to dry out naturally over a few weeks.

November: anemones

In the language of flowers, studied by the Victorians, the anemone meant 'forsaken'.

But I think that this is too melancholic for this bright woodland flower. I prefer to think the anemone is more hopeful and cheerful than that. It is certainly a flower that adds vibrant warmth and a splash of colour to winter weddings.

"A flower that spoke my language, and could tell
Of all the woods and ways my heart remembers well"
Edith Nesbit

Tisbury USA

We are asked to send some of our china and a customer's hand-knitted blanket to the customer's friend who lives in America. We discover that in Martha's Vineyard there is another Tisbury and also a Chilmark. Chilmark is a village near to us that we often deliver flowers to. It makes me wonder what Tisbury and Chilmark USA are like.

November in the florists' pub

Follow the high street up the hill out of Tisbury and the lane will take you along the edge of the valley as you make your way to the neighbouring village of Hindon. About half way along this path, on the outskirts of the small hamlet of Fonthill Gifford is the Beckford Arms.

If as you pass, you are tempted to call in to sit for a while in the sunny garden, or, in the winter, take shelter in the candlelight by the log fire, you might discover that the rest of the journey towards Hindon seems somehow less urgent or essential.

The road to the pub

And do not be surprised if, in a corner away from direct sunlight, you notice a stray florist or two recovering after a hard day's work

The pollen of lilies is poisonous for cats. So another good reason to remove the pollen of lily heads.

In November it is the landlady Karen's birthday. We are all asked to the party and are also asked to prepare some arrangements for the pub. We choose to mix dark-berried ivy with intense pink gerbera to reflect Karen's ability to successfully combine comfortable, worn antiques with modern splashes of colour.

flower shop secrets
PARTY FLOWERS

For an easy and striking flower arrangement crinkle cellophane into a tall glass vase, fill with water and then add a hand tied arrangement to the top. Flower heads can be placed in amongst the cellophane for extra effect.

Delivering to Manor Farm

December

December in the shop

With Christmas fast approaching we begin to receive deliveries of pine and ivy. One customer offers us some mistletoe and holly and on the way back from the florists' pub, after a quick break for a Christmas lunch, we call in to explore his extensive garden. He leaves his young son to negotiate the price so he has some extra pocket money for Christmas – and a good bargain is struck.

We prepare garlands and wreaths, there are baskets to be planted with bulbs and Christmas table arrangements to make up.

Getting ready for Christmas

A frequent and always welcome visitor throughout the year is Sarah, who buys gifts of flowers for the ladies she visits, old friends of her mum. She now orders a pretty Christmas wreath for her mum's graveside.

Pine and eucalyptus wreaths hung up ready for our customers

Christmas is a time for saying 'thank you', and we deliver a large bouquet to pub landlady Pat from a grateful customer, one of many such bouquets she receives during the year. When this customer first moved to England he fell on hard times but Pat showed she had faith in him which now, in happier times, he does not forget.

During a five-minute break we listen to carol singers from the village school who are raising money for Cancer Research in The Square outside the shop.

December: decorating the village church

We are called in to help decorate a local village church as there is to be a christening on the last Sunday before Christmas. The font is a mass of ivy, roses, cones and rich red apples.

The Empty Church

Blooming ladies snip and natter,
Miss Lane hushes 3 B chatter.
Tea-towel shepherds, tinsel kings,
Coat hanger angel wings.
Baby stirs with yawning mew,
Shuffling soles that tap the pew.
George's reading, squeaky, high,
Alleluias reach the sky.
Cool stone echoes where they stood,
Polished into cherry wood.

December: Christmas roses

At Christmas we include many red roses in our arrangements as they are so luxurious and festive. The traditional 'Christmas rose' or hellebore is a beautiful flower that we would like to use more often but sadly it is so delicate we find it does not last very long once cut.

We are busy with winter weddings. One bride chooses a bouquet of white roses splashed with vibrant purple lizzy. Whilst another chooses a small bouquet of red roses and red anemones mixed with ivy.

Black Bacarra

Passion

There are so many red roses to choose from. Here are three we love. Black Bacarra is so dark and soft it reminds me of black velvet. Passion is a strong beautifully shaped red rose, whilst Ruby Red has faded outer petals that give it an almost antique look.

flower shop secrets
ROSES

As a rule of thumb, the longer the stem, the fatter the head of the rose. So when you pay more for a long stemmed rose do not be afraid to cut it down if you want to. You are not wasting money by discarding the stem, your money has also been spent on the larger bloom.

Ruby Red in a bucket by some red spray roses

Town mouse, country mouse

My friend Nicky asks me to bring flowers to help decorate her apartment in Bath ready for Christmas. We unload mistletoe, arrangements of white roses and rose hips along with big bundles of amaryllis.

The table is set in the kitchen for a Christmas supper. Friends are coming to stay and to visit Bath Abbey where there will be a recital of Handel's Messiah. Around the corner from the abbey is the Christmas market which is inviting to explore with its mass of white fairy lights and the promise of mulled wine steaming the evening air.

December: amaryllis

Amaryllis cut flowers and plants wait in the shop ready to bloom for Christmas. It is not always easy to get the timing right and we move the plants in and out of the light so we will have the flowers ready for customers when they want them.

flower shop secrets
AMARYLLIS

Some amaryllis heads can be so heavy once the flowers are open that they are in danger of snapping or bending the stem. If you think this may happen put a stick up the hollow tube of the stem to give additional hidden support.

Christmas Eve in the shop

Everybody is in helping and the shop is crammed with customers. Rosie, our Saturday girl has been working all week, so has Hannah, who is back from university for the holidays.

Hannah brings in home-made mince pies and has written a poem called 'Working at Ted's' as her Christmas present to us all.

*"... Even though from time our sleep has been borrowed
I can't wait to come back for more tomorrow."*

Orders are collected or delivered. The butcher's wife picks up four bouquets her husband has ordered for the girls in their shop and she is delighted to find a fifth rather special bouquet he has arranged as a surprise for her. A driver arrives to collect flowers for a rock star and his film producer wife who are in the country for Christmas.

Jennifer hands out the last of the chocolates that have been in a vase by the till all week

The shop is swept and cleared. Eventually we close the door, we will not open again until the new year. On the way home to Christmas with our families there is one last delivery to make.

Delivering to Evelyn House

"Don't hurry, don't worry.
We are only here for a short visit
So be sure to stop and smell the flowers"
Walter Hagen